the decorative painter's
color shaper™
book

GLOUCESTER MASSACHUSETTS

QUARRY BOOKS

A Creative Guide for the Decorative Artist

Paula DeSimone

First published in the United States of America by
Quarry Books, an imprint of
Rockport Publishers, Inc.
33 Commercial Street
Gloucester, Massachusetts 01930-5089
Telephone: (978) 282-9590
Fax: (978) 283-2742

**Distributed to the book trade and art trade in the
United States by**
North Light, an imprint of
F & W Publications
1507 Dana Avenue
Cincinnati, Ohio 45207
Telephone: (800) 289-0963

Other Distribution by
Rockport Publishers, Inc.
Gloucester, Massachusetts 01930-5089

ISBN 1-56496-558-9

10 9 8 7 6 5 4 3 2 1

Design: The Design Company
Photography: Michael Lafferty
Printed in Hong Kong.

COLOR SHAPER™ and COLOUR SHAPER®
are registered trademarks of Forsline & Starr
International Ltd. For more information on the
COLOUR SHAPER®, call (908) 874-3315 in
the U.S., 44-1920-485-895 in the U.K.

contents

how to use this book

The Decorative Painter's Color Shaper Book is a guide to creating colorful patterns on a variety of surfaces through Color Shaping techniques. This book is designed to introduce you to a new and exciting approach to decorative painting. You will become acquainted with the Color Shaper through basic exercises and projects with easy to follow step-by-step instructions as well as pattern variations for each project. In addition, there are twenty-two patterns with recipes applicable to projects of your choice.

A variety of surfaces are introduced through the course of twelve projects. You will create beautiful patterns on wood, metals, ceramics, canvas, and paper. These surfaces are ideal for Color Shaping and make it possible to achieve polished results. The projects outlined in each section (brass planters, metal lamps, ceramic containers, tiles, lampshades, and so on) are readily available, and unfinished woodenware can be found in arts and crafts stores. Color Shaper sizes can be substituted if you do not have the specific size that is recommended in the materials list. Although the size of the stroke or motif will be different, you will still be able to create the pattern.

Unlimited possibilities will unfold as you discover the special effects of Color Shaping and translate creative thinking through technique.

basics

All of the projects in this book are created using the *Color Shaper*, a wonderful new painting tool from Forsline & Starr International Ltd. Color Shapers are rubber-tipped and come in a variety of sizes and shapes; they "move" paint easily to "carve" images in wet acrylic glaze. This exciting new tool simply lifts paint from the surface, leaving behind textures, forms, or lines. Combine simple Color Shaper marks, strokes, and squiggles to make sophisticated designs and patterns. A wonderful alternative to the paintbrush, the Color Shaper and a little imagination are all you need to create unique painted effects on whatever surface you choose.

This section introduces the basic family of tips for the five Color Shapers used throughout the book. From tapered points to angled edges, each type of Color Shaper comes in four sizes, and each tip makes its own distinctive mark. Get to know the different tips by copying the simple marks shown. With just a few minutes of practice, you'll achieve beautiful, polished results.

In the pages that follow, you'll learn to use Color Shapers to decorate tin, chrome, brass, wood, canvas, enamel, and even ceramic tile. But, to get started, practice the basic brushstrokes on plain paper, as they are shown here.

Color Shaper Tips

- The Color Shaper range includes five distinct tips, each in four sizes.
- The gray tip is best for this style of decorative painting: it offers good
- control in wet, acrylic glaze.
- Clean Color Shapers after use by dipping the tip in water and
- wiping.
- For stubborn stains, wipe the tip with a bit of alcohol or solvent.

color shaper sizes & shapes

The Color Shaper range includes five distinct tips, each in four sizes. The gray tip is ideal for this style of decorative painting: it offers good control in wet acrylic glaze. Clean Color Shapers after use by dipping the tip in water and wiping. For stubborn stains, wipe the tip with a bit of alcohol or solvent.

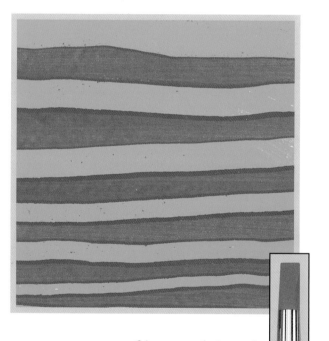

flat chisel
use for stripes and calligraphic strokes

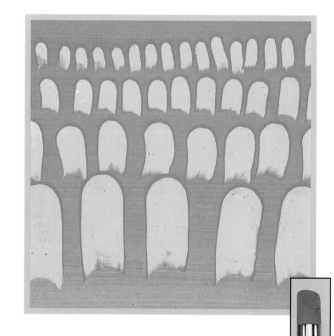

cup round
carves long and short rounded
strokes and petal forms

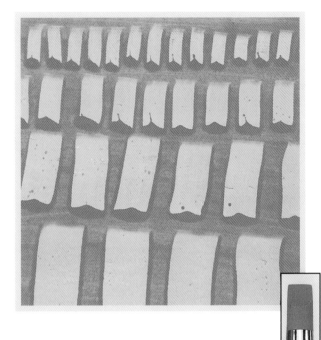

cup chisel
the concave tip carves well, ideal for
adjusting contours and edges

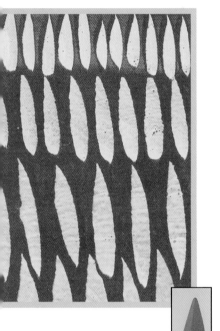

angle chisel
use the long, sharp edge for
broad to tapered expressive
strokes and leaf forms

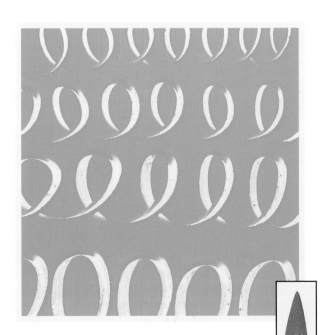

taper point
the tip makes linear strokes;
the side, broad marks

basic materials

These are some of the basic materials you will need to create the patterns and projects that follow. Most materials are available at arts and crafts stores, and some can also be found in paint and hardware stores.

Flow acrylic paint: Water-based paint with a pourable consistency that is ideal for decorative painting techniques (usually comes in two-ounce/59ml bottles).

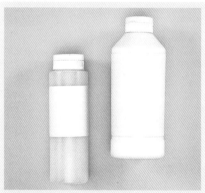

Extender: Water-based product that retards the drying time of paint. Ideal for making glazes used in Color Shaping techniques.

Glaze formula: Mix one part flow acrylic paint with one part extender. The extender increases the time the glaze will remain wet and workable for Color Shaping.

Color Shapers: Rubber-tipped tools in various sizes and shapes that are used to remove wet glaze through a calligraphic stroke technique to form designs and patterns.

Brushes: In addition to the Color Shapers, the projects use the following paint brushes: 1" (3 cm) wash brush, #12 flat shader brush, and #4 and #6 script liners.

Varnishing completed projects enhances and protects the finished project and produces a functional surface. A gloss or satin finish brings the colors in the patterns to life. The following steps are strongly recommended for wood and can be applied to metal. However, the wet-sanding process is not suggested for ceramic, canvas, or paper.

1. When the finished painted design is completely dry, gently apply several thin coats of water-based varnish with a soft bristle brush or sponge brush. Too much pressure when varnishing could disturb the delicate glazes. Apply at least three coats before beginning the next step.

2. Wet-sanding with #600 wet or dry sandpaper smoothes any imperfections in the finished surface and prepares it for subsequent layers. To wet-sand, cut a piece of #600 wet or dry sandpaper, dip it into mild soapy water and gently rub it over the decorated surface. Remove the soapy film with a damp paper towel and allow to air-dry. Varnish and wet-sand again. Repeat this process until the surface is perfectly smooth—on average, four or five times.

3. Apply the final coat of varnish. Do not wet-sand after the final coat. You may leave the sheen from the final coat of the satin or gloss varnish, or rub the surface very gently with #0000 steel wool for an eggshell finish.

Sandpaper: An assortment of grades is used in the projects, including #400 wet or dry sandpaper (for sanding between coats of paint in the preparation process) and #600 wet or dry sandpaper (used in the finishing, wet-sanding process).

Palette paper: Poly-coated paper with a slippery, waxy surface that is ideal for practicing Color Shaping techniques, experimenting with strokes, and serving as an effective background for applying wet glaze.

Spray acrylic or water-based varnish: Gloss or semi-gloss water-based varnish is used for all the projects, at several points:

- between layers of paint when creating backgrounds as a sealer that protects each layer;
- to seal the finished background before Color Shaping techniques are applied (at least three coats are needed to produce a slick surface appropriate for Color Shaping);
- over the completed project, to provide a smooth, protective finish (several coats are needed and each coat should be allowed to dry thoroughly).

Primer: Used to prepare the surface of unfinished wood projects before either backgrounds or Color Shaping techniques are applied.

basic brushstrokes

The range of Color Shaper sizes and tips can produce a variety of strokes. Combine simple lines, dots, and squiggles to form a number of patterns and designs; achieve more calligraphic-like effects through stroke techniques. For example, use the Flat Chisel to create the *S* stroke, spiral, and scroll. The Angle Chisel is ideal for leaf and petal designs, and the Cup Round is perfect for making dotted marks. The size of the tip determines the size of the stroke. Experiment and become familiar with the variety of the Color Shapers to expand the range and possibilities of creativity. A sampling of strokes and simple patterns are presented here.

Use the tip of the Cup Round to create dotted marks. Combine these strokes to form a simple, repetitive pattern.

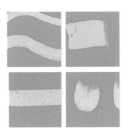

lines, squiggles, and dots

The Flat Chisel produces simple short and long lines as well as the squiggle line.

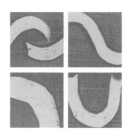

c u r v e s

The Flat Chisel is used to form simple to complex curvilinear strokes, ranging from a *U* shape to a reverse curve.

Create a horizontal *S* border or an interlocking *S* stroke with the Flat Chisel.

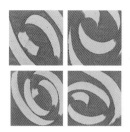

spirals and scrolls

Spirals and scrolls are created with the Flat Chisel. Experiment with the horizontal or vertical direction of the stroke to form a variety of designs.

leaves and petals

The Angle Chisel is ideal for forming leaf and petal strokes.
Combine a series of strokes to complete a motif. The Angle Chisel
can create anything from simple leaves to complex ferns or from primitive to stylized flowers.

working with
metals

Metal items of tin, chrome, brass, and enamelware have smooth, finished surfaces that are fast and easy to decorate. Most metals need no preparation; acrylic glazes glide right on and can be patterned very quickly with a Color Shaper. Best of all, metal lets you experiment and try different patterns over and over on the same object. Just rinse off the glaze while it is still wet, wipe dry, and begin again until you reach the desired effect.

There are many hues and textures of metal to choose from—the range of options includes the golden brilliance of brass and the sparkling silver of smooth chrome and tin. Enamelware adds color or plain white to the picture. If you choose a brass surface, try to find "treated" brass to avoid tarnish with age. And, whatever metal you work with, seal the finished artwork with spray acrylic varnish. Don't worry if you cannot find an exact match for the drum container, plate, lampshade, and footed pot featured in the step-by-step projects that follow. Keep in mind that the brushstrokes and patterns adapt readily to many different sizes and shapes.

chrome spiral canister

Containers are perfect first projects and come in lots of interesting forms. The simple lines and small size of this canister make it easy to work with and complement the repetitive, allover spiral design.

Starting Out

You may want to prepare a simple sketch to arrange the design elements or you may wish to be spontaneous and just start to paint.

Remember, the advantage of a metal surface is that you can try different glazing and shaping techniques without harming the background. Simply rinse off the glaze and begin again!

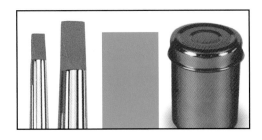

materials

chrome drum container

#2 and #6 Flat Chisel Color Shapers

1" (3 cm) wash brush

turquoise flow acrylic paint

water-based extender

spray acrylic varnish

{1}

Prepare a glaze by mixing one part turquoise flow acrylic paint with one part extender. Using the wash brush, apply the glaze to the chrome surface in sections.

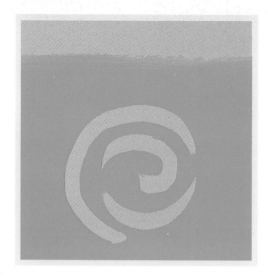

{2}

Work on the "body" of the container first, then the lid. With the #6 Flat Chisel Color Shaper, shape spiral designs randomly into wet glaze. The spirals shown are made with three nested crescent strokes.

{3}

Make simple stripes in a circle on the lid by shaping the wet glaze with the #6 Flat Chisel Color Shaper. Wipe the Color Shaper every few stripes to keep glaze from building up on the tip. Keep the stripes the same length and evenly spaced.

{4}

Create a spiral border on the outside edges of the lid by using the #2 Flat Chisel Color Shaper. The "end" of each spiral should point down toward the bottom of the container. Or for a more "active" design, alternate the spirals so that every other spiral points upward. Seal with varnish.

glaze tip

If you find that the glaze is beading up, try gently sanding the project with #600 wet or dry sandpaper. The slightly rougher surface will help the paint adhere.

variation

Once you have completed the project, you may wish to explore other simple motifs. This reverse curve stroke is done with the #6 Flat Chisel Color Shaper and forms a random pattern.

{1}

Prepare a glaze by mixing one part fuchsia flow acrylic paint with one part extender. Using the wash brush, apply the glaze to the chrome surface in sections.

{2}

With a #6 Flat Chisel Color Shaper, carve a spiral with a long *S* curve ending in another spiral, as shown. The beginning of the spiral may be two separate strokes, but try to make the *S* curve with a single, fluid motion. Seal completed pattern with varnish.

patterned enamel plate

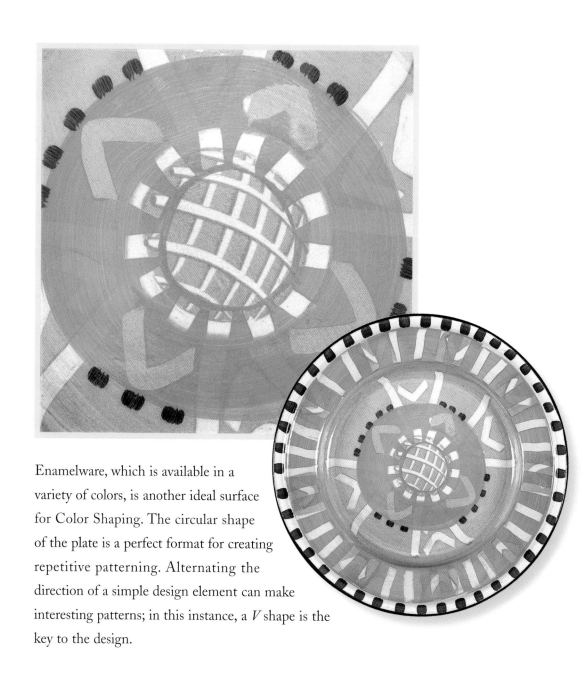

Enamelware, which is available in a variety of colors, is another ideal surface for Color Shaping. The circular shape of the plate is a perfect format for creating repetitive patterning. Alternating the direction of a simple design element can make interesting patterns; in this instance, a *V* shape is the key to the design.

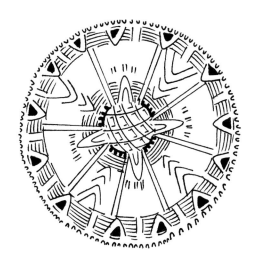

Starting Out

As this project pattern has a repetitive nature, it is a good idea to create a design layout before painting.

Draw a circle on a sheet of paper. Within this circle, draw a series of concentric circles. Arrange a series of Vs and simple marks to form a pattern.

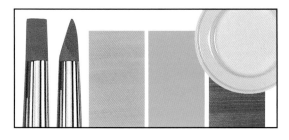

materials

enamel plate

#6 Flat Chisel and #6 Angle Chisel Color Shapers

1" (3 cm) wash brush

#4 script liner

flow acrylic paint in yellow, turquoise,
    and ultra blue

water-based extender

spray acrylic varnish

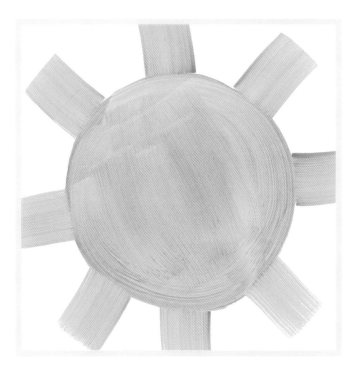

{1}

Prepare a glaze by mixing one part yellow flow acrylic paint with one part extender. Using the wash brush, apply the glaze to the flat area of the plate first. Then, using the same brush, create a stripe around the outer edges.

{3}

Mix a glaze of one part turquoise flow acrylic paint and one part extender. With the wash brush, form a doughnut shape in the center and paint the turquoise glaze around the band. Using the #6 Flat Chisel Color Shaper, form additional *V*s in the alternating spoke areas, reversing the direction of the *V*. Make straight strokes around the edge of the inner circle and around the band. You may choose to complete the doughnut area before proceeding with the band. Seal with varnish.

{2}

With the #6 Flat Chisel Color Shaper, carve a center circle into the wet glaze. Pull straight strokes from the circle to create a spoke effect. Continue the pattern by forming *V*s within the narrow spoke areas and on each yellow stripe around the border. Working quickly while the glaze is wet, shape a crisscross center using the tip of the #6 Angle Chisel Color Shaper. Let dry. Seal with three coats of varnish, allowing the project to dry thoroughly between coats.

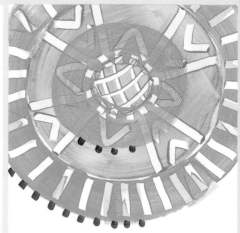

{4}

Using the #4 script liner, paint a series of dotted strokes with ultra flow blue acrylic paint to form a finished edge by pressing down with the tip of the brush. Try adding a few dotted strokes around the doughnut shape as well. Complete the project with several coats of varnish to give the project a protective, polished finish.

glaze tip

Use a circular motion, following the shape of the plate, when applying the glazes.

variation

Experiment with similar approaches to design and vary your palette. Continue to explore the *V* shape as a design element.

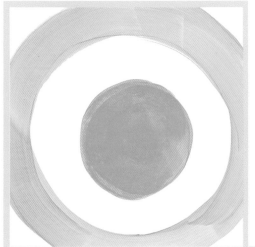

{1}

Prepare a glaze by mixing one part yellow flow acrylic paint with one part extender. With the wash brush, paint a small circle in the center of the plate and a band toward the outer edge. Seal with three coats of varnish.

{2}

Prepare a glaze by mixing one part fuchsia flow acrylic paint with one part extender. With the wash brush, paint a fuchsia band around the inner yellow circle and the outside edge, overlapping some of the yellow and white areas. With the #6 Flat Chisel Color Shaper, create *V*s in alternating directions. Seal with three coats of varnish.

{3}

The final glaze consists of one part turquoise flow acrylic paint and one part extender. With the wash brush, paint two bands around the inner yellow circle and fuchsia bands, overlapping the yellow, white, and fuchsia areas. With the #6 Flat Chisel Color Shaper, create straight strokes, forming a striped pattern within each band. You can add dotted edges to the design by dipping the tip of the #4 script liner in blue-violet flow acrylic paint and pressing down with the brush to create a dotted mark. Seal design with varnish.

sunflower metal lampshade

Old and new metal lamps can be found in a variety of styles. This particular lamp, which was purchased in bright green, came in an assortment of colors—all of them perfectly suitable backgrounds for Color Shaping techniques. With a light source behind it, this pattern will be especially lovely.

Starting Out

Sketch your ideas on paper to determine the number of flowers for the size of the lampshade.

Use equal spacing when laying out the pattern to avoid running out of room when forming the last flower.

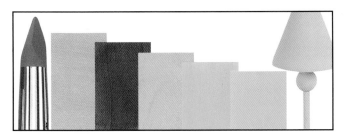

materials

metal lamp

#6 Angle Chisel Color Shaper

1" (3 cm) wash brush

#12 flat shader brush

#4 script liner (or narrow brush of your choice)

flow acrylic paint in yellow-orange,

    light magenta, light blue-violet, coral,

    and grape

rubber stoppers or corks for printing circles

water-based extender

spray acrylic varnish

{1}

Using the wash brush, paint vertical stripes in yellow-orange around the lampshade. (Note that the green here is the color of the lamp purchased; yours may differ.)

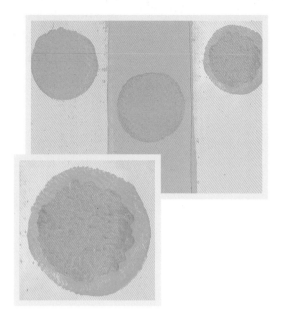

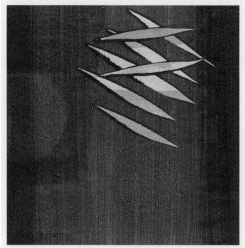

glaze tip

When applying glaze in sections, do not overlap wet glaze over dry glaze. This will create an uneven effect. Instead, try to line up each section of glaze right next to the previous one.

{2}

Apply coral flow acrylic paint directly to a rubber stopper or cork and stamp over the striped background. Load fresh paint for each impression. Let dry, then stamp smaller light magenta circles directly over larger coral ones in the same manner. Let dry, and seal with a coat of varnish.

{4}

Prepare a glaze by mixing one part grape flow acrylic paint with one part extender. With the wash brush, apply the glaze in sections over the entire surface of the lampshade. Using the #6 Angle Chisel Color Shaper, make a crisscross center.

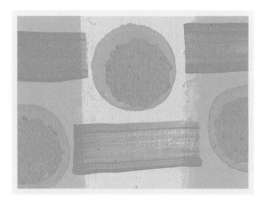

{3}

With the #12 flat shader brush, paint short horizontal strokes in light blue-violet between each of the circles, forming a repetitive pattern. Switch to the #4 script liner or other narrow brush and paint horizontal stripes in coral on the yellow-orange stripes. Let dry. Apply three coats of varnish.

{5}

While the glaze is still wet, shape petals around the center with the #6 Angle Chisel Color Shaper. For the petal stroke, put pressure on the angle edge of the Color Shaper and push away. Let dry thoroughly. Apply four to five coats of varnish to finish the project.

variation

To make an allover pattern on a lampshade, carve a loose scroll or ribbon stroke, accented by black *V*s.

{1}

With the wash brush, paint vertical lilac stripes around the lampshade. Using the #12 flat shader brush, paint horizontal light orange stripes over the first set of stripes, forming a plaid. Let dry. (You may wish to seal this step with a coat of varnish.) With the #4 script liner or another narrow brush, paint vertical stripes spaced evenly over the background (use your eye to judge the spacing). Let dry and seal with three coats of varnish.

{2}

Prepare a glaze by mixing one part light purple flow acrylic paint with one part extender. With the wash brush, apply the glaze in sections. With the #6 Flat Chisel Color Shaper, carve a scroll stroke. The image looks like an inverted *J* motif. Apply a coat of varnish. Using a medium-point indelible black marker, form *V*s in the negative space of the design. Finish with varnish.

brass pot scrolls

The brilliance of brass is revealed through the magic of Color Shaping. Like the other metals, its smooth surface allows the rubber tips to glide easily and create beautifully contoured edges. A variety of brass objects are readily available and make perfect projects for Color Shaping. The scrolls on the sides of this round pot give it special character.

Starting Out

Mirror-image designs can create interesting patterns when used in Color Shaping. The pattern used in this project is an example of a mirror image where two scrolls face opposite directions.

To achieve these designs, practice on palette paper first to refine the design.

materials

brass pot

#10 Flat Chisel Color Shaper

   (#6 Flat Chisel would work well also)

1" (3 cm) wash brush

#6 script liner (or narrow brush of your choice)

flow acrylic paint in blue-violet, black,

   and white

water-based extender

spray acrylic varnish

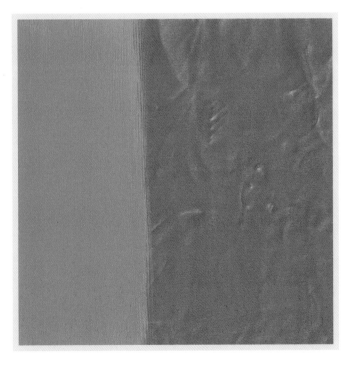

{1}

Prepare a glaze by mixing one part blue-violet flow acrylic paint with one part extender. Using the wash brush, apply the glaze in sections.

scroll tip

Experiment with Color Shaping

techniques on palette paper.

This will allow you to develop

the scroll technique on a flat

surface before applying it to a

rounded surface.

{2}

With the #10 Flat Chisel Color Shaper, carve a set of two vertical straight strokes into the wet glaze. (Notice how easily the Color Shaper glides through the wet glaze.) Hold the Color Shaper at a slight angle and apply firm, even pressure for a clean sweep.

{3}

Again using the #10 Flat Chisel Color Shaper, create a pair of scroll strokes that line up next to the first series of straight strokes. Manipulate the Color Shaper in the same manner to control the evenness of the strokes. Repeat the glazing and shaping steps until the pattern covers the entire project. Once the pattern has been completed, finish painting the underside of the pot with the remaining blue-violet glaze.

{4}

With the #6 script liner or another narrow brush, paint a series of straight brushstrokes with white flow acrylic paint around the top edge of the pot to form a border. Load the brush with white paint evenly on both sides, flattening it to form consistent strokes. Repeat this process using black flow acrylic paint, filling in the spaces between the white strokes to form a black-and-white border. Seal with varnish.

variation

Explore other combinations of scroll designs to form patterns. The *S* design is used as a continuous band in the variation.

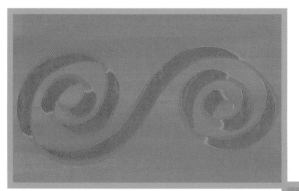

{1}

Prepare a rich glaze by mixing one part blue flow acrylic paint with one part extender. Using the wash brush, apply the glaze in sections as before. With the #10 Flat Chisel Color Shaper, create a horizontal *S*-like spiral. Use firm, even pressure to control the stroke. Form a repetitive design; try to maintain equal sizing and spacing.

{2}

Shape horizontal bands with the broad-tipped #16 and #10 Flat Chisel Color Shapers. You may substitute smaller Color Shapers and create several narrower bands instead of broad ones. Paint a black-and-white striped edge by following the directions in step 4 of the brass pot project. Seal with varnish.

working with
wood

Unlike metal surfaces, wood must be prepared to achieve a smooth surface for the Color Shaping techniques to be effective. Surface preparation, then, is extremely important when working on unfinished wood. Initially, sand the wood to a refined finish, using a variety of grades of sandpaper. If the surface is rough, begin sanding with a medium grade, such as #150, and move progressively toward #400 wet or dry sandpaper.

Priming unfinished wood ensures that the later applications of paint and varnish adhere properly. After sanding, apply one or two coats of a good-quality primer, and sand with #400 wet or dry sandpaper between and after each coat.

After the primer has dried, apply a colored basecoat. Select a background color to suit your design. For smaller projects, use flow acrylic paint; for larger ones, try a good-quality flat latex paint. Two coats of base color are recommended, sanding with #400 wet or dry sandpaper between coats and after the final basecoat. Coat the finished surface with spray acrylic varnish. All backgrounds should be sealed with a minimum of three coats of varnish, drying thoroughly between coats, before the Color Shaper techniques are applied.

rings & checks
candlestick

Wooden candleholders can be found in styles ranging from traditional to contemporary. This particular example is broad-based and allows plenty of room for surface decorating. If the candleholder you choose is narrower, experiment with smaller motifs for its design.

Starting Out

Because it is more difficult to "erase" an unwanted stroke on wood than it is on metal, plan the design by creating a simple line drawing.

Use your design to create a clear picture for spacing and repeating shapes.

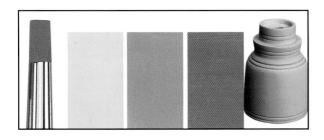

materials

unfinished wooden candleholder

primer

#6 Flat Chisel Color Shaper

1" (3 cm) wash brush

flow acrylic paint in lime green,
    light magenta, and red-orange

water-based extender

water-based varnish

sandpaper in assorted grades

{1}

Prepare wood surface as directed on page 36, using lime green as the basecoat color. Seal with a coat of varnish.

{2}

Create a checkerboard pattern by painting squares with the wash brush in light magenta. Practice a few times on palette paper to achieve equal sizes and spaces. Paint the trim colors at this time. Seal with three coats of varnish before proceeding.

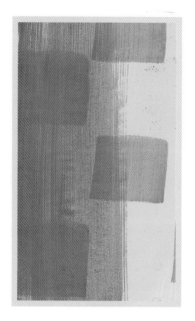

{3}

Prepare a glaze by mixing one part red-orange flow acrylic paint with one part extender. Using the wash brush, apply the glaze in sections in a vertical direction.

{4}

With the #6 Flat Chisel Color Shaper, shape doughnuts into the wet glaze, forming an overall pattern. Notice the interesting design that is created. Dry thoroughly and proceed with the finishing process as directed on page 11 in the Basic Materials section.

spacing tip

Use the width of the brush as a guide for the spacing for the checkerboard; a simple brushstroke will create the check.

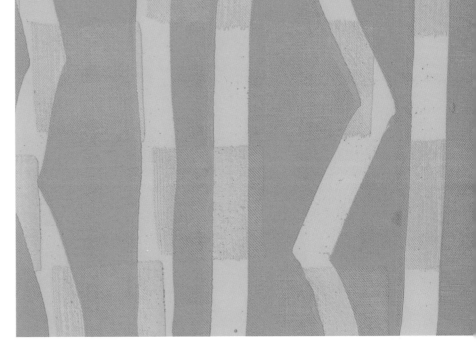

variation

Experiment with a variety of color combinations, again using the check pattern as the underlayer. Glazing on top with transparent color can create some pleasing color changes.

{1}

Following wood preparation directions, prepare a sea aqua background. Seal this step with a coat of varnish. Then, follow step 2 from the wooden candleholder project using yellow-orange flow acrylic paint.

{2}

Prepare a glaze by mixing one part hot pink flow acrylic paint with one part extender. Using the wash brush, apply the glaze in sections in a vertical direction. With a #10 Cup Chisel Color Shaper (you may wish to experiment with other sizes and shapes), form stripes and zigzags in a vertical direction into the wet glaze. Varnish and finish as directed.

zigzag picture frame

Frames make great projects, whether you choose to insert a mirror or a favorite photo. A painted frame could serve as an extension to a painting with some creative thinking; the range of sizes and shapes is unlimited. Look for a frame that is fairly wide to allow for more surface decoration. The *V*s in this design accentuate the geometric shape of the object.

Starting Out

It is always a good idea to sketch your design on paper first.

Give careful consideration to designs that involve a right angle. Notice how half of the V shape anchors the four corners of the frame.

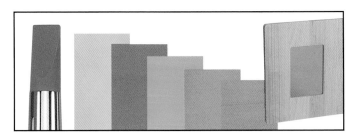

materials

unfinished wooden frame

primer

#10 Flat Chisel Color Shaper

1" (3 cm) wash brush

#12 flat shader brush

flow acrylic paint in yellow ochre,

    light rust, pink, grape, and turquoise

rubber or foam circles for stamping

water-based extender

water-based varnish

sandpaper in assorted grades

{1}

Prepare wood surface as directed, using yellow ochre as the base color. Seal with a coat of varnish. Paint 1" (3 cm) stripes horizontally and vertically with the wash brush in light rust flow acrylic paint. Cover all sides of the frame. Try to match the placement of the stripes to create a symmetrical layout. Seal with a coat of varnish.

{2}

Apply pink flow acrylic paint directly to rubber or foam circles with the #12 flat shader brush and stamp on the prepared background. Load the paint neatly for each impression. Create an overall pattern with a random, tossed effect. Seal with another coat of varnish.

{3}

Continue in the same manner of stamping, using a smaller circular stamp with grape flow acrylic paint. Some overlap adds interest to the design. Seal this step with three coats of varnish.

design tip

After anchoring the four corners with the first set of strokes, complete those *V*s before continuing to shape the remaining *V*s. This will help to distribute the design evenly.

{4}

Prepare a glaze by mixing one part turquoise flow acrylic paint with one part extender. Using the wash brush, apply the glaze to the prepared frame in sections.

{5}

With the #10 Flat Chisel Color Shaper, shape *V*s on all sides of the frame in alternating directions. Begin by forming half of the *V* in each of the four corners. This will establish a guideline. Use firm pressure and control the straight edges of the strokes for consistent shapes. Continue completing the *V* patterning until all four sections are shaped. Finish as directed on page 11 in the Basic Materials section.

variation

Try an alternative approach by using a white background and substituting a *U* shape for the *V* shape.

{1}

Prepare a white background (follow wood preparation directions on page 36) and varnish to seal. Apply spring green flow acrylic paint to a rubber or foam circle and stamp all over surface. Apply a coat of varnish. Cover a small rubber circle with blue flow acrylic paint; stamp, overlapping some of the green circles. Apply three coats of varnish to seal.

{2}

Prepare a glaze by mixing one part grape flow acrylic paint with one part extender. Using the wash brush, apply the glaze to wood surface in sections. With the #10 Flat Chisel Color Shaper, carve *U* shapes into the wet glaze. Finish as directed.

leaf motif box

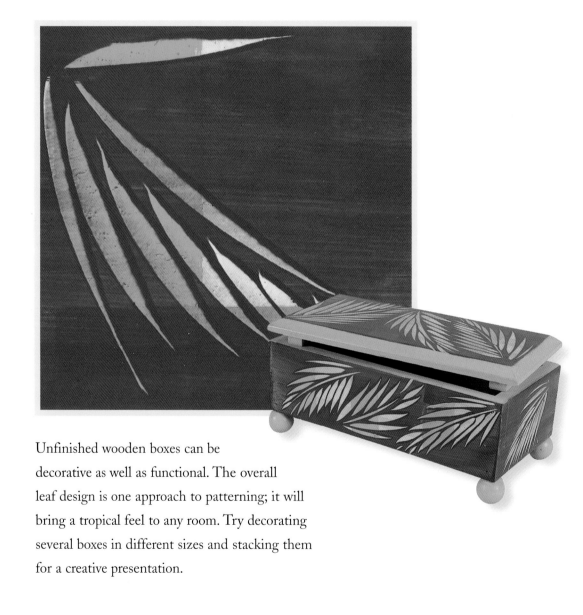

Unfinished wooden boxes can be decorative as well as functional. The overall leaf design is one approach to patterning; it will bring a tropical feel to any room. Try decorating several boxes in different sizes and stacking them for a creative presentation.

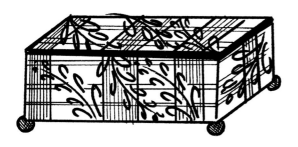

Starting Out

Prepare a simple sketch to arrange the leaves.

Practice making leaf shapes on palette paper with the Angle Chisel Color Shaper.

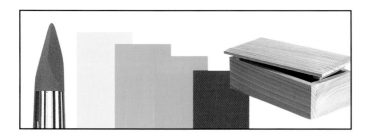

materials

unfinished wooden box

primer

#10 Angle Chisel Color Shaper

1" (3 cm) wash brush

#12 flat shader brush

flow acrylic paint in yellow, turquoise,

    spring green, and wine

water-based extender

water-based varnish

sandpaper in assorted grades

{1}

Prepare wood surface as directed in opener, using yellow as the basecoat. Be certain to apply a layer of varnish after the final yellow coat is applied. Next, apply the plaid background by painting evenly spaced, vertical turquoise stripes with the wash brush on the top and sides of the box. You might want to establish the center stripe first, then continue to stripe accordingly. Apply a coat of varnish to seal.

color tip

Select a harmonious color to accent the trim; in this case, turquoise paint was applied. Painted turquoise wooden balls were glued to the box's underside to create feet.

{2}

Using the #12 flat shader brush, paint a series of horizontal green stripes over the turquoise ones, creating a layered effect. This step completes the plaid background. Apply three coats of varnish. Each coat must be thoroughly dry before applying the next.

{4}

With the #10 Angle Chisel Color Shaper, establish the center vein of the leaf and then form leafy strokes on both sides of it, starting from the bottom up; the angle of the tip creates the shape of the leaf. Use even pressure. When the pattern is complete, finish as directed.

{3}

Prepare a glaze by mixing one part wine flow acrylic paint with one part extender. Using the wash brush, apply the glaze over the plaid background.

variation

Experiment with a variety of plaid backgrounds and glazes to form new and interesting designs. The same fern pattern used on the wooden box was re-created here using different colors.

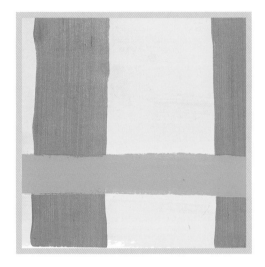

{1}

Prepare a yellow background (follow wood preparation instructions). Apply vertical lavender stripes using the wash brush, letting the width of the brush form the stripe. Seal with a coat of varnish. Paint ¹/₂" (1 cm) horizontal turquoise stripes over the vertical set, using the #12 flat shader brush. Seal with three coats of varnish.

{2}

Prepare a glaze by mixing one part fuchsia flow acrylic paint with one part extender. Using the wash brush, apply the glaze on top of the plaid background in sections. With the #10 Angle Chisel Color Shaper, create the leaves as in step 4 of the wooden box project. Notice the interesting color changes that occur. Finish as directed.

cross band
tray

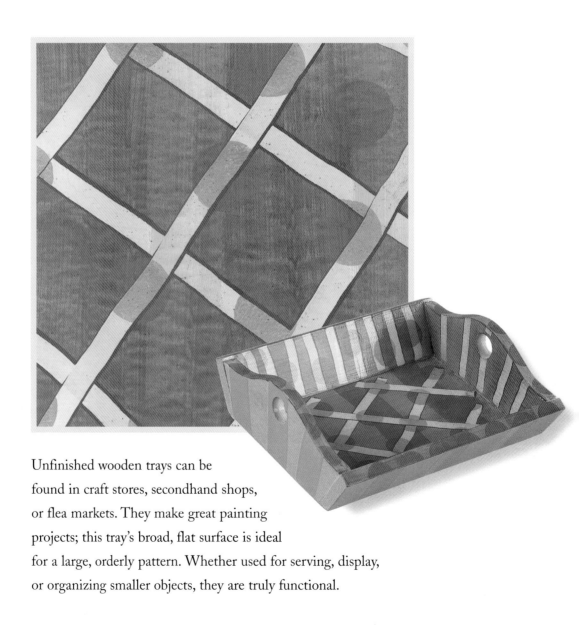

Unfinished wooden trays can be
found in craft stores, secondhand shops,
or flea markets. They make great painting
projects; this tray's broad, flat surface is ideal
for a large, orderly pattern. Whether used for serving, display,
or organizing smaller objects, they are truly functional.

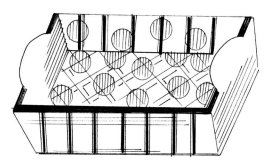

Starting Out

Sketch a design on paper that will complement the shape of the tray.

Prepare the wood as directed on page 36 to ensure the best possible results.

materials

unfinished wooden tray

primer

#10 Flat Chisel Color Shaper

1" (3 cm) wash brush

flow acrylic paint in butterscotch yellow,

    turquoise, lilac, and orange

rubber stopper or cork for stamping

water-based extender

water-based varnish

sandpaper in assorted grades

{1}

Prepare a butterscotch yellow background. With the wash brush, paint vertical stripes in turquoise flow acrylic paint, letting the width of the brush form the width of the stripe.

{2}

Apply lilac flow acrylic paint directly to a rubber stopper or cork and stamp circles all over the background. For a clear stamped image, apply a fresh coat of paint for each impression. Seal with three coats of varnish.

{3}

Prepare a glaze by mixing one part orange flow acrylic paint with one part extender. With the wash brush, apply the glaze over the entire flat area of the tray.

{4}

While the glaze is wet, use the #10 Flat Chisel Color Shaper to form a cross band pattern. The only way to neatly achieve the crisscross pattern is to do it all at once. You need to work quickly, as there is only so much time before the glaze sets up. Try to space the lines evenly to create a consistent diamond pattern. Finish glazing in orange around the sides of the tray, one section at a time, forming stripes with the Color Shaper. Follow the finishing instructions on page 11 in the Basic Materials section.

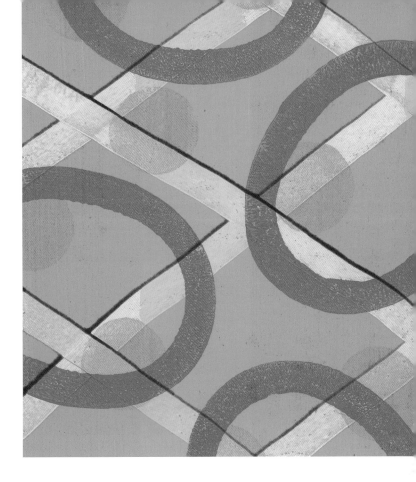

v a r i a t i o n

Experiment with a variety of cross band designs and stamps, such as this coffee mug holder pattern.

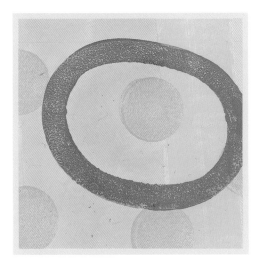

{1}

Prepare a butterscotch yellow background with turquoise stripes and stamped lilac circles as directed in the wooden tray project. Apply purple flow acrylic paint to the opening of a foam coffee mug holder and stamp rings around the circles. Seal with three coats of varnish.

{2}

Prepare a glaze by mixing one part deep teal flow acrylic paint with one part extender. Apply the glaze over the surface as previously directed. Using the #10 Flat Chisel Color Shaper, create the cross band pattern as described in step 4 of the wooden tray project. Refer to the instructions for the finishing process on page 11 in the Basic Materials section.

working with ceramics

Ceramic objects and tiles are ideal for applying Color Shaping techniques. No preparation is necessary, and the range of available objects is extensive, from plant pots to tiles and accessories. The advantage is that you can experiment on the same project with glazing and Color Shaping, developing and perfecting your skills and techniques as many times as you like without destroying the surface. Because the ceramic has been fired, wet glaze can easily be removed by cleaning it off with soapy water.

Bringing painted surfaces into contact with food is not recommended. If you wish to decorate serving pieces, consider painting only the outside of the object, such as the outside of a bowl or a pitcher. Finished projects should be coated several times with water-based varnish or spray acrylic varnish. Be certain that each coat is thoroughly dry before applying the next.

ceramic tile
swirls

Tiles are wonderful first projects for
experimenting on ceramics. Because they
are flat, they are easy to handle, and the
slippery surface is perfect for glazing
and sliding the Color Shapers. The tile
featured here is white, but you may want
to explore other color combinations.

Starting Out

Try sketching several ideas on paper before beginning to paint.

Use a square format to develop your drawing so it will proportionately relate to the tile and make it easy to transfer the design.

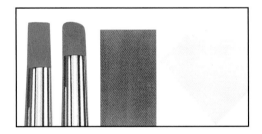

materials

ceramic tile

#6 Flat Chisel and #6 Cup Round Color Shapers

1" (3 cm) wash brush

ultra blue flow acrylic paint

rubber combing tool

water-based extender

water-based varnish or spray acrylic varnish

{1}

Prepare a glaze by mixing one part ultra blue flow acrylic paint with one part extender. Using the wash brush, apply the glaze evenly over the entire surface of the tile.

varnish tip

To match the sheen of the

ceramic tile, use a high-gloss

varnish after you Color Shape

your pattern.

{2}

With the rubber combing tool, comb a 1" (3 cm) border around the outside of the tile, intersecting at the four corners. Use a firm but even pressure, holding the comb on a slight angle.

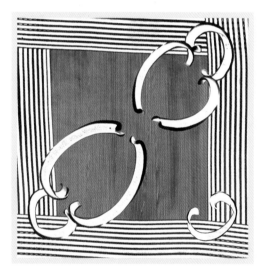

{4}

Working quickly while the glaze is still wet, create petal-like strokes around the edges of each of the four large petals using the #6 Cup Round Color Shaper. Holding the Color Shaper flat, press down and push away from you. Notice the gradation that results from this stroke. When dry, apply several coats of water-based varnish or spray acrylic varnish.

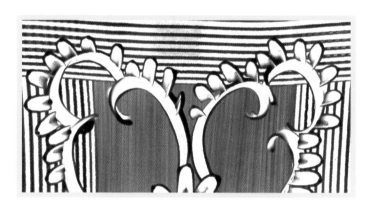

{3}

While the glaze is still wet, Color Shape four large petals with the #6 Flat Chisel Color Shaper (or you may wish to use a larger Color Shaper). Use the four corners of the tile to guide you in placing the petals. Begin with the smallest curved stroke to form the tip, then add the two side strokes to complete the petal. Angle the Color Shaper slightly to control the stroke.

variation

Explore similar designs while incorporating some new Color Shaping techniques. If you are intrigued by the effects of the blue-and-white palette, look to Oriental porcelains and Dutch designs for inspiration.

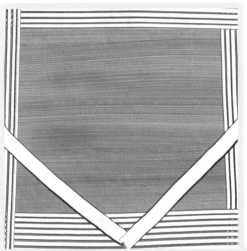

{1}

Prepare a blue glaze as directed in step 1 of the ceramic tile project. With the rubber combing tool, comb a 1" (3 cm) border around the outside edge of the tile. Working quickly, Color Shape a diamond with the #6 Flat Chisel Color Shaper. You may like to experiment with a broader tip.

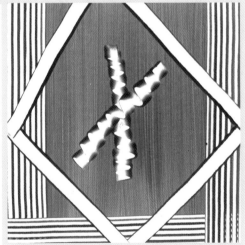

{2}

With the #6 Flat Chisel Color Shaper, make squiggles in the center area to form a flower motif. Each squiggle should intersect at the same point to form the center of the flower. Complete the flower by dipping your little finger into the wet glaze and stamping a dot in the center. Finish as directed in step 4 on page 58.

crisscross scroll container

Ceramic containers are ideal Color Shaping projects; their surfaces, like that of ceramic tiles, are smooth, glossy, and easy to work on. Find an object with an appealing size and shape and let those elements dictate the design. This pattern's elegant scrolls and swirls add formal accents to the plain container.

Starting Out

Prepare a sketch on paper that combines simple scrolls with crisscross lines to form a pattern. The sketch will give you an idea of the number of scrolls that will fit evenly around the container.

Look to Oriental porcelain as a great source of inspiration for design ideas.

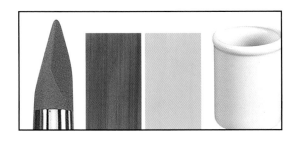

materials

ceramic container

#10 Angle Chisel Color Shaper

1" (3 cm) wash brush

flow acrylic paint in deep blue-violet
   and yellow-orange

water-based extender

water-based varnish or spray acrylic varnish

{1}

Prepare a glaze by mixing one part deep blue-violet flow acrylic paint with one part extender. Using the wash brush, apply the glaze to the ceramic surface in sections. (The sections of the glaze should relate to the size of the design unit for the pattern. Complete each section before moving on to the next.) With the #10 Angle Chisel Color Shaper, create two vertical scrolls that are mirror images of each other, forming a cartouche, a kind of ornamental frame.

{3}

Working quickly, use the #10 Angle Chisel Color Shaper to pull small delicate spirals from the large scrolls (you may wish to use a smaller Angle Chisel Color Shaper). When the first cartouche is complete, continue to glaze and Color Shape the remaining cartouches.

{2}

While the glaze is still wet, use the #10 Angle Chisel Color Shaper to form a diagonal crisscross pattern within the cartouche.

varnish tip

When applying the initial

coat of varnish over the

completed glazed pattern, use

a very thin coat. Try not to

apply too much pressure when

spreading; excess varnish and

pressure could lift the glaze.

{4}

Paint a yellow-orange band around the top of the container. Let the project dry thoroughly before varnishing. Four to five coats are recommended for a tough finish.

variation

Try a two-layered approach for a variation.

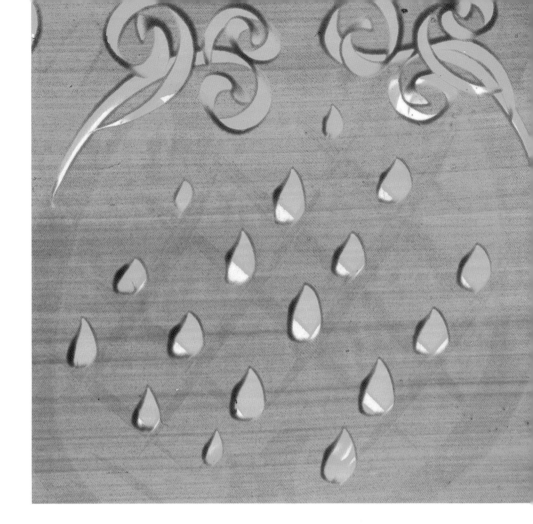

{1}

Prepare a glaze by mixing one part turquoise flow acrylic paint with one part extender. Using the wash brush, apply the glaze to the ceramic surface in sections. Create the same scroll cartouches used in the chinoiserie project, including the crisscross center. Let dry thoroughly and apply three coats of varnish.

{2}

Prepare a glaze by mixing one part deep blue flow acrylic paint with one part extender. Apply the glaze in sections with the wash brush. Notice how the white scrolls have turned light blue from the glaze.

{3}

With the #10 or #6 Angle Chisel Color Shaper, create small spirals and scrolls from the larger scroll. While the glaze is still wet, make teardrop strokes with the #10 or #6 Angle Chisel Color Shaper within the crisscross section; press down and lift to form the teardrop. Seal with varnish.

working with

canvas & paper

Primed canvas and coated, laminated, or varnished paper
are all ideal surfaces for Color Shaping. Primed canvas
(preferably floorcloth-weight) can be cut into place mats
or table runners. You can find canvas-covered sketchbooks
and notebooks in craft stores. Such paper surfaces as
lampshades and journals are also suitable for Color
Shaping. However, the painted background needs to
be varnished at least three times beforehand; a slick,
nonporous surface is necessary for effective results.

paper lampshade designs

Coated paper lampshades have polished surfaces that work well with Color Shaping techniques. Or, with some creative planning, Color Shaped patterns can enhance an already existing lamp base. The playful design on this lampshade will quickly become a treasured accent for almost any style of decor.

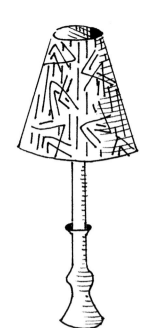

Starting Out

Sketch a few ideas on paper to organize possible design elements.

To see how your design works on a three-dimensional form, bend the paper to simulate the lampshade shape and simply staple it.

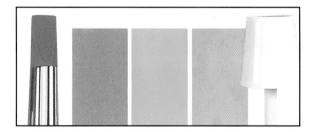

materials

coated paper lampshade

#6 Flat Chisel Color Shaper

1" (3 cm) wash brush

#12 flat shader brush

flow acrylic paint in light magenta, lilac,

   and red-orange

medium-point indelible black marker

water-based extender

water-based varnish or spray acrylic varnish

{1}

With the #12 flat shader brush, paint vertical stripes in light magenta on the lampshade. Seal with a coat of varnish.

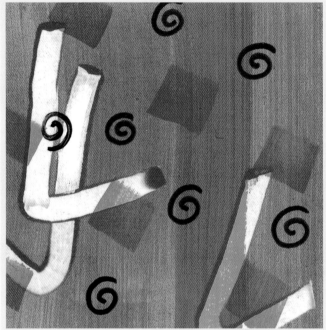

varnish tip

On a piece of scrap paper or cardboard, test the marker with a coat of varnish to be certain that no smudging will occur.

{2}

From a diagonal direction, paint short strokes with the #12 flat shader brush in lilac flow acrylic paint, forming an allover pattern. Seal with three coats of varnish.

{4}

You may choose to take the design a step further. Using a medium-point indelible black marker, draw spirals over the Color Shaped pattern. Apply several coats of varnish to seal and protect the lampshade.

{3}

Prepare a glaze by mixing one part red-orange flow acrylic paint with one part extender. With the wash brush, apply the glaze in sections over the prepared background. With the #6 Flat Chisel Color Shaper, create an allover, interlocking *V* pattern. Let dry thoroughly and seal with a coat of varnish.

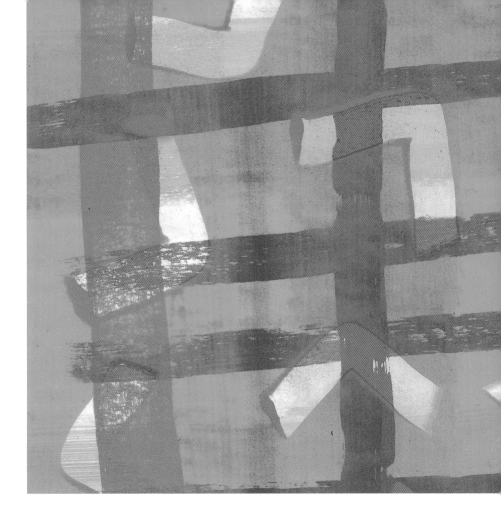

variation

Experiment with a variety of painted backgrounds and colors, such as this plaid pattern.

{1}

Prepare a plaid background. Paint vertical stripes with the wash brush in golden yellow. Let dry and seal with a coat of varnish. Then paint horizontal stripes in olive green with the wash brush. Let dry and seal with a coat of varnish. Using the #12 flat shader brush, paint vertical stripes in light purple, and seal this step also.

{2}

With a #4 script liner, paint horizontal and vertical stripes in hot pink. The plaid is complete; seal the background pattern with three coats of varnish. Prepare a glaze by mixing one part blue-green flow acrylic paint with one part extender. With the wash brush, apply the glaze in sections and Color Shape *V*s with the #10 Flat Chisel Color Shaper. Seal with varnish.

scrolls & spirals
place mats

Primed canvas floorcloth is
ideal for place mats. The
weight is functional and it
can be cut into a variety of sizes
and shapes depending on the
desired effect. In addition to the standard
rectangle, try out other shapes, such as an oval
or a hexagon. The curved, flowing lines of this
pattern add interest to the strict geometric
shape of the surface.

Starting Out

On paper, sketch your design before painting.

Use a sharp pair of scissors to cut the edge of the place mat cleanly. Varnish the raw edges to prevent them from fraying.

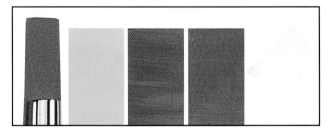

materials

primed canvas floorcloth cut into an 11" x 17"

   (28 cm x 43 cm) piece

#10 Flat Chisel Color Shaper

1" (3 cm) wash brush

flow acrylic paint in white, yellow, magenta,

   and blue-violet

rubber combing tool

water-based extender

water-based varnish or spray acrylic varnish

{1}

Apply a basecoat of white flow acrylic paint over entire place mat and let dry. Even though your primed canvas is already white, it is still important to use a basecoat for a more permanent finish. Seal it with a coat of varnish. Using the wash brush, paint a series of large commas in yellow flow acrylic paint. Create a random, tossed effect. With the wash brush, freely paint some leaves around each of the large commas. Seal with three coats of varnish.

scroll tip

Try a practice sheet of painted yellow scrolls. When forming the stroke, think of a very large comma as a guide.

{2}

Prepare a glaze by mixing one part magenta flow acrylic paint with one part extender. With the wash brush, apply the glaze in sections over the prepared background. Quickly comb small sections randomly with the rubber combing tool on the wet glaze.

{3}

While the glaze is still wet, use the #10 Flat Chisel Color Shaper to form spirals through the combed sections, completing the individual design. Continue to glaze, comb, and shape in sections until the entire place mat is covered. Let dry thoroughly and seal with a coat of varnish.

{4}

Prepare a glaze by mixing one part blue-violet flow acrylic paint with one part extender. With the wash brush, paint a broad stripe with the glaze at each end of the placemat. Notice the interesting change in color. If you choose, you can create the stripes with masking tape for perfectly straight edges. The completed place mat should have four to five coats of varnish for a durable and functional surface.

variation

Experiment with other large shapes for background patterns.

{1}

Paint large, semi-abstract floral shapes in yellow flow acrylic paint. Apply turquoise flow acrylic paint directly onto a rubber stopper or cork and stamp circular centers into the flowers. Then stamp orange circles in the spaces between the flowers. Seal with three coats of varnish.

{2}

Prepare a glaze by mixing one part red-violet flow acrylic paint with one part extender. Using the wash brush, apply the glaze evenly over the sealed pattern in sections. With the #10 Flat Chisel Color Shaper, create a spiral, making first the center of a flower then the outside petals by forming alternating *V*s around the spiral. Cover the surface with the design and seal with varnish.

pattern recipes

confetti squiggles

Color Shaping a transparent glaze over a simple striped background produces interesting effects.

to create this pattern you will need:

#6 Flat Chisel Color Shaper

1" (3 cm) wash brush

#12 flat shader brush

flow acrylic paint in yellow, peach, pink, and turquoise

water-based extender

water-based varnish

{1}

Paint a yellow basecoat and let dry. With the #12 flat shader brush, paint vertical peach stripes. Alternate with pink stripes painted with the wash brush, until the entire surface is striped. Let dry. Apply three coats of water-based varnish to seal the pattern. Do not skip the varnish step—it is important not only to seal the striped background but also to produce a slick surface for Color Shaping.

{2}

Mix a glaze of one part turquoise flow acrylic paint and one part extender and apply with the wash brush. Carve squiggles into the wet glaze with the #6 Flat Chisel Color Shaper. You may want to try this first in sections. Experiment to create other simple marks and shapes. When the design is complete, seal with a coat of varnish.

line dance

Color and shape come together to create a pattern full of movement and excitement.

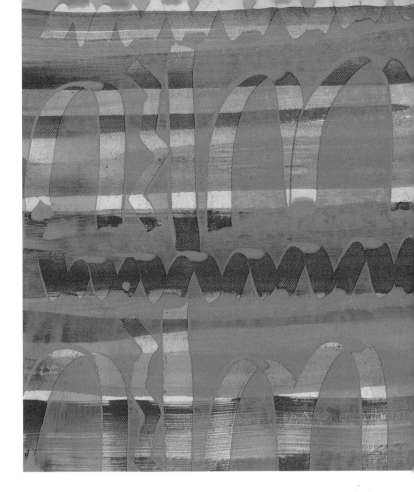

{1}

Paint a white basecoat. Let dry and seal with a coat of varnish. It's best to stripe over a varnished background because the paint slides nicely, and any "accidents" can be wiped away with a swipe of a damp paper towel. With the wash brush, paint a series of alternating vertical stripes in yellow, orange, and pink. Use a free painting style for striping. Apply three coats of varnish to seal the striped background.

to create this pattern you will need:

#10 Flat Chisel Color Shaper

1" (3 cm) wash brush

flow acrylic paint in white, yellow, orange, pink, and blue

water-based extender

water-based varnish

{2}

Mix a glaze of one part blue flow acrylic paint and one part extender and apply evenly with the wash brush in sections. With the #10 Flat Chisel Color Shaper, create long squiggles to section off broad, striped areas. Within each striped section, Color Shape a series of *N*s, zigzags, stripes, and *M*s in a horizontal, repetitive pattern. Let dry, and seal completed design with varnish.

tropical leaves

For variety, create a whole forest of ferns by overlapping the Color Shaped patterns on their striped background.

{1}

Paint a pink basecoat. Let dry. Seal background with a coat of varnish. With the wash brush, paint alternating vertical stripes in yellow and blue. Apply three coats of varnish to seal the striped pattern.

{2}

Mix a glaze of one part magenta flow acrylic paint and one part extender. With the wash brush, apply glaze over striped background in sections. Using the tip of the #10 Angle Chisel Color Shaper, create the structural form of a fern. Then continue to shape small leafy strokes on each side of the structure. This approach helps to arrange the strokes evenly and naturally. Be certain to press down and push away with the tip of the Color Shaper. Continue the pattern and let dry. Seal with varnish.

to create this pattern you will need:

#10 Angle Chisel Color Shaper

1" (3 cm) wash brush

flow acrylic paint in pink, yellow, blue,

   and magenta

water-based extender

water-based varnish

to create this pattern you will need:

#16 Angle Chisel Color Shaper

(a #10 will produce a smaller motif)

1" (3 cm) wash brush

flow acrylic paint in apricot, turquoise, and magenta

varnish

fern grove

In this pattern, the delicate shapes of the fern leaves provide a striking contrast to the striped background.

{1}

Paint an apricot basecoat and let dry. Varnish to seal background. With the wash brush, paint vertical stripes in turquoise flow acrylic paint, spacing evenly. Apply three coats of varnish.

{2}

Mix a glaze of one part magenta flow acrylic paint and one part extender. With the wash brush, apply evenly over the striped background in sections. Establish the center veins first, then create leafy strokes with the #16 Angle Chisel Color Shaper to form large ferns. Let dry. Varnish to seal the completed pattern.

cross bands

Cross band designs are wonderful on all sorts of decorative projects. This is one example of a such pattern, in which parallel lines intersect to form a grid.

{1}

First, create a freestyle plaid background. Paint a pale lavender basecoat and let dry. With the #12 flat shader brush, paint vertical lemon yellow stripes, then add horizontal orange stripes with the wash brush. Next, use the #12 flat shader brush to apply vertical red and light green stripes over the first two sets of stripes. Let dry and seal with three coats of varnish.

{2}

Mix a glaze of one part blue flow acrylic paint, one part extender, and apply to broad areas with the wash brush. With the #10 Cup Chisel Color Shaper, squiggle evenly spaced diagonal lines in one direction. Repeat in the opposite direction. The results are quite interesting. Varnish to seal the completed pattern.

to create this pattern you will need:

#10 Cup Chisel Color Shaper

1" (3 cm) wash brush

#12 flat shader brush

flow acrylic paint in lemon yellow, red,

orange, pale lavender, light green,

and blue

water-based extender

water-based varnish

banded checks

A check pattern is a great way to explore Color Shaping techniques. Again, plaid serves as a background.

to create this pattern you will need:

#6 Flat Chisel Color Shaper

1" (3 cm) wash brush

#12 flat shader brush

flow acrylic paint in yellow, mint green,

    light blue, turquoise, white, and purple

rubber combing tool

water-based extender

water-based varnish

{1}

First, paint a freestyle plaid background. Over a white basecoat, paint vertical yellow stripes, then add horizontal turquoise stripes with the wash brush. Paint vertical mint-green stripes with the wash brush, then add vertical and horizontal light blue stripes with the #12 flat shader brush. Seal with three coats of varnish. (It is also fun to experiment with plaid combinations of your own.)

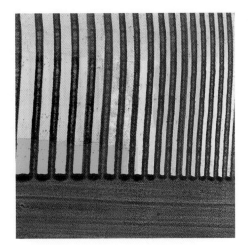

{2}

Mix a glaze of one part purple flow acrylic paint and one part extender, and use the wash brush to cover the plaid background with glaze. Create the checkerboard effect shown by combing in squares the width of the rubber combing tool. Space squares evenly, and work quickly before the glaze has a chance to set. Varnish to seal.

{3}

Between the combed squares, use the #6 Flat Chisel Color Shaper to carve a zigzag stroke resembling an abstract tree. Seal with varnish.

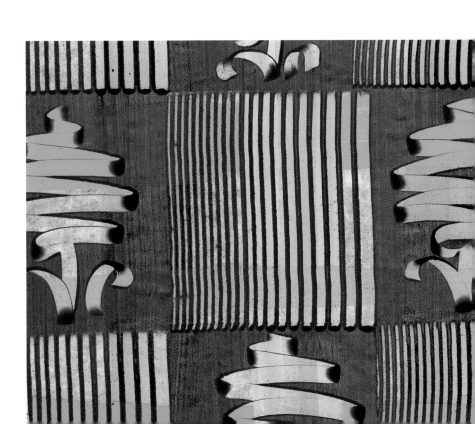

falling leaves

A plaid background enhances glazing and shaping techniques. Notice the range of colors produced in the leaf pattern.

to create this pattern you will need:

#10 Angle Chisel Color Shaper

1" (3 cm) wash brush

#12 flat shader brush

flow acrylic paint in yellow, orange, blue-violet, violet, and pink

water-based extender

water-based varnish

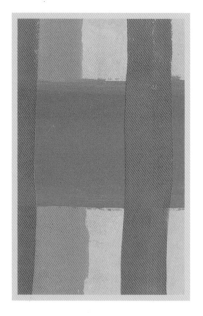

{1}

Create the plaid background first. Paint a yellow basecoat and let dry. Using the wash brush, add vertical pink stripes and horizontal blue-violet stripes. With the #12 flat shader brush, paint vertical orange stripes over the pink and blue-violet bands. Let dry. Seal with three coats of varnish.

{2}

Mix a glaze of one part violet flow acrylic paint and one part extender, and apply with the wash brush (it may be easiest to do this in sections). With the angle edge of the #10 Angle Chisel Color Shaper, make random leaf-shaped strokes to create an overall pattern. Notice the contour edges of the strokes. Let dry, and seal with a coat of varnish.

dots and daisies

Combining stamped images as a background for Color Shaping unleashes an infinite number of possibilities for creative patterning. A foam toe spacer used in nail painting makes a wonderful abstract stamp. Rubber or foam tubes create great round stamps.

to create this pattern you will need:

#10 Cup Round and #6 Taper Point Color Shapers

1" (3 cm) wash brush

flow acrylic paint in yellow, coral, turquoise, and red-violet

foam toe spacer

rubber or foam tubes

water-based extender

water-based varnish

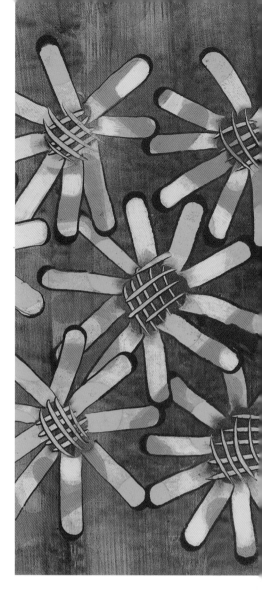

{1}

Paint a yellow background (do not varnish). Begin stamping by applying coral flow acrylic paint directly to foam toe spacers. Press directly on yellow background to create a stamped image. Repeat this process until you have scattered this image all over the surface. Use a rubber or foam tube to stamp on turquoise flow acrylic paint in the same manner. Varnish with three coats to seal.

{2}

Mix a glaze of one part red-violet flow acrylic paint and one part extender. With the wash brush, apply glaze over sections of the stamped background. Imagine the center of a flower. With the #10 Cup Round Color Shaper, push from the center of your imaginary flower outward, creating a petal-like shape. Continue in this manner until you have created complete flower forms. Don't hesitate to overlap; it adds interest to the design.

{3}

While the center areas are still wet, use the #6 Taper Point Color Shaper to create a crisscross center. Varnish to seal.

paint with numbers

Color Shaping over a stamped background produces creative results. Found objects in rubber and foam make great stamping tools. In this pattern, a foam coffee mug holder was used to produce the oval stamped shapes.

{1}

To prepare the stamped background, apply a pink basecoat and let dry. Do not varnish—you'll get much better images by stamping over a non-varnished surface. To use the oval opening of a foam coffee mug holder as a stamp, apply terra cotta flow acrylic paint directly to its edge with the #12 flat shader brush (or any small brush) and stamp directly on the pink background. Repeat to create an overall pattern, then seal with three coats of varnish.

{2}

Mix a glaze of one part blue-green flow acrylic paint and one part extender and apply with the wash brush. While the glaze is wet, shape the numbers *1*, *2*, and *3* randomly with the #10 Flat Chisel Color Shaper to create a pattern, or try letters as an alternative. Seal completed design with varnish.

to create this pattern you will need:

#10 Flat Chisel Color Shaper

1" (3 cm) wash brush

#12 flat shader brush

flow acrylic paint in pink, terra cotta,

and blue-green

foam coffee mug holder

water-based extender

water-based varnish

letter block pattern

Under a glaze of Color Shaped letters, stamps of children's letter blocks or *U*-shaped foam create a pattern with surprising depth.

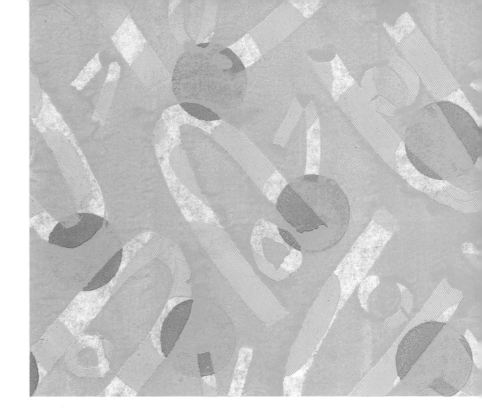

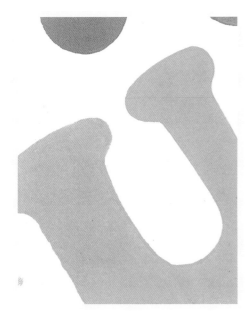

{1}

Apply a white basecoat and let dry (do not varnish background). With the wash brush, apply apricot flow acrylic paint directly to a *U*-shaped block and stamp onto the background. Create an overall pattern of *U* stamps, loading fresh paint before each impression. Next, apply coral flow acrylic paint to a circular stamp in the same manner and create a random, tossed effect. Seal pattern with three coats of varnish.

{2}

Mix a glaze using one part turquoise flow acrylic paint with one part extender. With the wash brush, apply glaze evenly over pattern in sections. While the glaze is wet, Color Shape *U*s with the #10 Flat Chisel Color Shaper and smaller *O* and *V* shapes with the #6 Flat Chisel Color Shaper. Let dry and seal completed design with varnish.

to create this pattern you will need:

#6 and #10 Flat Chisel Color Shapers

1" (3 cm) wash brush

flow acrylic paint in white, apricot, coral, and turquoise

foam or rubber stopper or cork foam or rubber children's letter block

water-based extender

water-based varnish

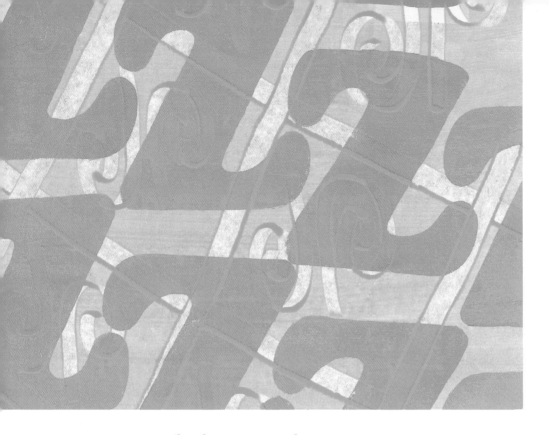

to create this
pattern you will
need:

#6 and #10 Flat Chisel Color Shapers

1" (3 cm) wash brush

flow acrylic paint in white, coral,

   and spring green

foam or rubber children's *Z* letter block

water-based extender

water-based varnish

z and diamond pattern

The familiar becomes somehow unfamiliar as the letter *Z* takes on new life as a zigzag stamp design element in this pattern.

{2}

Mix a glaze of one part spring green flow acrylic paint and one part extender. Apply glaze evenly with the wash brush, covering a broad area. Working quickly, Color Shape cross bands with the #10 Flat Chisel Color Shaper. While the glaze is still wet, shape a *J*-inverted *J* motif with the #6 Flat Chisel Color Shaper within each diamond shape. Let dry and seal with varnish.

{1}

Apply a white basecoat and let dry. With the wash brush, apply coral flow acrylic paint directly to the *Z* block and stamp, forming a diagonal pattern. Use your eye to space and line up the *Z*s. Seal with three coats of varnish.

checks and stripes

This pattern also involves Color Shaping over a stamped background, and it must be created quickly before the glaze has time to dry.

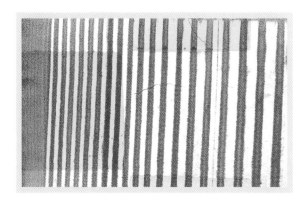

{2}

Mix a glaze of one part magenta flow acrylic paint and one part extender. With the wash brush, apply glaze evenly and in sections over the stamped background. While the glaze is wet, form a vertical stripe with the rubber combing tool. Working quickly, use the #10 Flat Chisel Color Shaper to form alternating *V*s through the combed pattern. Add squiggles to each side of the combed stripe with the #10 Flat Chisel Color Shaper. Repeat the process, continuing to form the pattern. Let dry thoroughly and seal with varnish.

{1}

Prepare a white basecoat and let dry. Apply lime green paint to a square block and create a checkerboard pattern. Seal with three coats of varnish.

to create this pattern you will need:

#10 Flat Chisel Color Shaper

1" (3 cm) wash brush

flow acrylic paint in white, lime green, and magenta

rubber combing cool

foam or rubber square block

water-based extender

water-based varnish

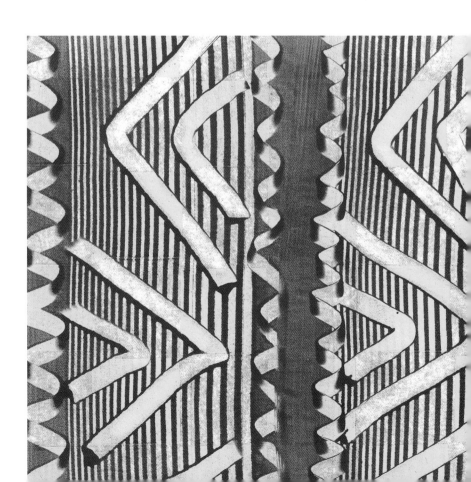

arches and stripes

Stamping, combing, and Color Shaping combine in this unusual design. Try different sizes of Color Shapers and observe their effects on the final design.

to create this pattern you will need:

#10 Flat Chisel Color Shaper

1" (3 cm) wash brush

rubber combing tool

flow acrylic paint in lime green,

deep blue-green, and fuchsia

foam or rubber triangles

water-based extender

water-based varnish

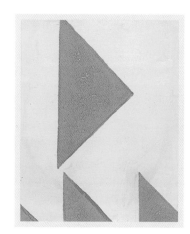

{1}

Prepare a lime green basecoat and let dry. Apply deep blue-green flow acrylic paint directly to the triangle block and stamp. Load paint for each impression. Try to evenly space and line up the triangles in a striped pattern. Seal with three coats of varnish.

{2}

Mix a glaze of one part fuchsia flow acrylic paint and one part extender. Apply evenly with the wash brush over stamped background in sections. While the glaze is wet, comb a checkerboard pattern and immediately Color Shape *V*s with the #10 Flat Chisel Color Shaper right through the wet combing. Let dry thoroughly and seal with varnish.

scrolls over dots and blocks

Despite its simple elements, this design intrigues the eye and gives it much to consider with the various levels incorporated within.

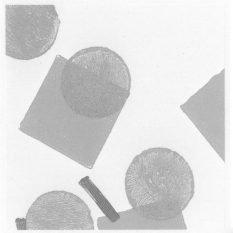

{1}

Prepare a lemon yellow basecoat and let dry. Do not varnish. Apply turquoise flow acrylic paint directly to the square foam or rubber block with the wash brush and stamp onto the yellow background. Create a random, tossed effect. Next, apply pink flow acrylic paint directly to the round stopper or cork and stamp, scattering the circles and overlapping some of the square stamps. With the #4 script liner, paint terra cotta lines in all directions directly over the stamped background. Seal with three coats of varnish.

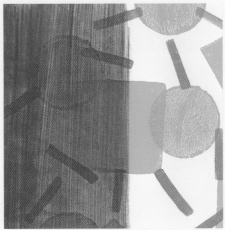

{2}

Mix a glaze of one part plum flow acrylic paint and one part extender, and use the wash brush to apply the glaze in sections. While the glaze is wet, Color Shape interlocking *C* scrolls randomly with the #10 Flat Chisel Color Shaper (you may wish to practice the stroke a bit first on palette paper). Glaze and Color Shape in sections. Notice the transparent effects after the glaze is applied. Seal completed pattern with varnish.

to create this pattern you will need:

#10 Flat Chisel Color Shaper

1" (3 cm) wash brush

#4 script liner

flow acrylic paint in lemon yellow,

    turquoise, pink, terra cotta, and plum

foam or rubber square block

round stopper

water-based extender

water-based varnish

spiral bouquets

Another pattern uses a large children's block of the letter *O* to create an interesting floral design. Experiment with other colors, too.

to create this pattern you will need:

#6 Flat Chisel Color Shaper

1" (3 cm) wash brush

flow acrylic paint in light olive, turquoise, and blue

foam or rubber children's *O* letter block

water-based extender

water-based varnish

{1}

Prepare a light olive basecoat and let dry. Apply turquoise flow acrylic paint directly to the *O* block and stamp repeatedly to create an overall pattern. Seal with three coats of varnish.

{2}

Mix a glaze of one part blue flow acrylic paint and one part extender. With the wash brush, apply glaze in sections over stamped background. While the glaze is wet, create a cluster of small spirals with the #6 Flat Chisel Color Shaper. Then immediately shape lines around the cluster, forming petals. Continue glazing and Color Shaping to create a floral pattern. Varnish to seal.

stripes, circles, and petals

Explore Color Shaping over painted patterned backgrounds. Go beyond simple stripes and stamps—experiment with brushstrokes to create background designs.

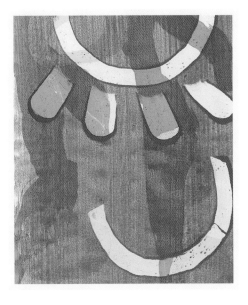

{2}

Mix a glaze of one part purple flow acrylic paint and one part extender. With the wash brush, apply glaze evenly over prepared background in sections. Using the #6 Flat Chisel Color Shaper, create half-circles and scrolls resembling paper clips in the wet glaze. Then use the #10 Cup Round Color Shaper to create petal strokes around the half-circles. To create the petal stroke, push down with firm pressure and then away from you using the tip of the Color Shaper. Seal completed pattern with varnish.

to create this pattern you will need:

#6 Flat Chisel and #10 Cup Round
   Color Shapers

1" (3 cm) wash brush

#6 script liner

flow acrylic paint in pale green,
   coral, lime green, and purple

water-based extender

water-based varnish

{1}

Paint a pale green basecoat and let dry, then seal with a coat of varnish. With the #6 script liner, paint irregular vertical stripes in coral flow acrylic paint. Continue patterning by painting irregular circular shapes in lime green with the #6 script liner, overlapping the striped background. Apply three coats of varnish to seal pattern.

water flowers

The stripes and colors used in this pattern recall woodgrain, but the glaze of turquoise flowers layered over it creates a watery effect.

{2}

Mix a glaze of one part turquoise flow acrylic paint and one part extender. Apply glaze with the wash brush over pattern in sections. While the glaze is wet, shape spirals with the #6 Flat Chisel Color Shaper. Next, use the #10 or #6 Angle Chisel Color Shaper to form petals around the spirals. Push down firmly and then away with the edges of the Color Shaper, for a clean petal stroke. Create a random, tossed effect. Seal completed pattern with varnish.

{1}

Paint a yellow-orange basecoat. Let dry and seal with a coat of varnish. With the #6 script liner, paint irregular vertical stripes in coral flow acrylic paint. Create circular shapes within striped sections in light turquoise with the #6 script liner and outline some of the curved stripes. Apply three coats of varnish to seal the pattern.

to create this pattern you will need:

#10 or #6 Angle Chisel Color Shaper

#6 Flat Chisel Color Shaper

1" (3 cm) wash brush

#6 script liner

flow acrylic paint in yellow-orange, coral, light turquoise and turquoise

water-based extender

water-based varnish

paisley and scroll pattern

The creative freedom involved in Color Shaping is reflected in this use of the traditionally staid paisley pattern over a freehand patterned background.

{1}

Prepare a yellow-olive basecoat. Let dry and varnish to seal. With the wash brush, create a pink paisley pattern over the basecoat color by making big comma-shaped strokes. Let dry. Paint smaller comma-shaped strokes in orange on top of the pink stroke with the #6 script liner. Add dots in orange and light magenta, edging the paisley design. Let dry and varnish to seal. Outline the paisleys with indelible black marker (first, test marker on scrap paper to make sure it does not bleed under varnish). Seal completed background with three coats of varnish.

{2}

Prepare a glaze of one part grape flow acrylic paint and one part extender. Apply with the wash brush over the patterned background in sections. Using the #6 Flat Chisel Color Shaper, create *S*-like scrolls in the wet glaze. Practice the strokes on palette paper to get the calligraphic style. While the glaze is still wet, use the #6 Cup Round Color Shaper to form short petal strokes, edging the scrolls. Seal the completed design with varnish.

to create this pattern you will need:

#6 Flat Chisel and #6 Cup Round
    Color Shapers

1" (3 cm) wash brush

#6 script liner

flow acrylic paint in yellow-olive, pink,
    orange, light magenta, and grape

medium-point indelible black marker

water-based extender

water-based varnish

Color Shaped lattice

Color Shaping over this freehand patterned background produces a pattern that is attractive when used on large flat surfaces such as tabletops.

to create this pattern you will need:

#6 and #10 Flat Chisel Color Shapers

1" (3 cm) wash brush

#12 flat shader brush

flow acrylic paint in mint green, aqua, lilac, blue-violet, and bright coral

water-based extender

water-based varnish

{1}

Prepare a mint green basecoat. Let dry, and then seal with varnish. With the wash brush, randomly paint irregular circular shapes in aqua and allow to dry. Overlap similar shapes in lilac. Repeat a smaller shape in blue-violet using the #12 flat shader brush, once again overlapping other shapes. Seal with three coats of varnish.

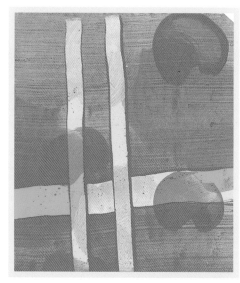

{2}

Mix a glaze of one part bright coral flow acrylic paint and one part extender. Apply with the wash brush in sections over the patterned background. With the #10 Flat Chisel Color Shaper, create vertical stripes in the wet glaze. While the glaze is still wet, switch to the #6 Flat Chisel Color Shaper and shape horizontal stripes, forming a grid-like pattern. Quickly form *V*s in alternating directions with the #6 Flat Chisel Color Shaper. Seal completed pattern with varnish.

hot and cold strokes

Short vertical and horizontal strokes formed by the Color Shaper uncover a freehand pattern underneath a red-orange glaze.

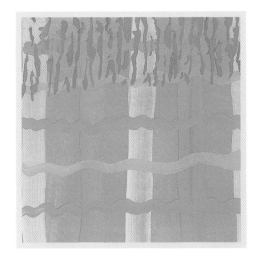

{1}

Paint a yellow ochre basecoat. Let dry, and seal background with a coat of varnish. With the #12 flat shader brush, paint alternating vertical stripes in light cobalt blue and pale yellow. Use your eye to determine spacing; the width of the brush creates the width of the stripe. With the #4 script liner, paint long squiggly lines in light terra cotta on top of the striped background. Seal this step with varnish. With the #4 script liner, paint short jagged lines in medium cobalt blue over the entire pattern. Seal with three coats of varnish.

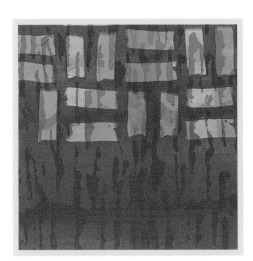

{2}

Mix a glaze of one part red-orange flow acrylic paint and one part extender. Evenly apply glaze over patterned background with the wash brush in sections. Notice the transparent effects and color changes that occur. With the #6 Flat Chisel Color Shaper, create pairs of short horizontal and vertical strokes forming a repetitive pattern. Seal design with varnish.

to create this pattern you will need:

#6 Flat Chisel Color Shaper

1" (3 cm) wash brush

#12 flat shader brush

#4 script liner

flow acrylic paint in yellow ochre,

   light and medium cobalt blue,

   pale yellow, light terra cotta,

   and red-orange

spring ribbons

Color Shaping over a cellophaned background results in a subtle pattern that emphasizes the scroll shapes.

to create this pattern you will need:

#6 Flat Chisel Color Shaper

1" (3 cm) wash brush

flow acrylic paint in lime green, turquoise, and light violet

plastic sandwich wrap

water-based extender

water-based varnish

{1}

Paint a lime green basecoat. Let dry, and seal with a coat of varnish. It is important to varnish basecoat color before applying the plastic sandwich wrap.

{3}

Mix a glaze of one part light violet flow acrylic paint and one part extender. Apply in sections over the prepared textured background with the wash brush. With the #6 Flat Chisel Color Shaper, create a cluster of curly scrolls within a striped format; letting them intersect one another. Seal the completed design with varnish.

{2}

Mix a glaze of one part turquoise flow acrylic paint and one part extender. Apply the glaze over the sealed basecoat with the wash brush. Quickly place a sheet of crinkled plastic wrap over the wet glaze and press down gently. Peel the wrap off carefully, and notice the interesting pattern that results. Let dry, and seal with three coats of varnish.

lines, *c*, and zigzags

Once you have mastered the basic techniques in glazing and Color Shaping, you may wish to further experiment with layering Color Shaped designs to form more complex patterns.

to create this pattern you will need:

#10 Flat Chisel Color Shaper

1" (3 cm) wash brush

flow acrylic paint in pink, light turquoise, lavender, orange, and magenta

water-based extender

water-based varnish

{1}

Prepare a pink basecoat. Let dry and seal with a coat of varnish. With the wash brush, paint alternating vertical stripes in light turquoise and lavender. Seal with three coats of varnish.

{2}

Mix a glaze of one part orange flow acrylic paint and one part extender. Apply over striped background in sections with the wash brush. Using the #10 Flat Chisel Color Shaper, shape a motif into the wet glaze that combines a *C*, a line, and a zigzag. Let dry and seal with three coats of varnish.

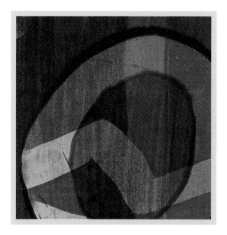

{3}

Prepare a glaze of one part magenta flow acrylic paint and one part extender. Apply with the wash brush in sections, and create circles with the #10 Flat Chisel Color Shaper. Notice the interesting transparent effects and color changes. Varnish to seal.

acknowledgments

I would like to extend my appreciation to Forsline & Starr International for developing a series of tools that have inspired me to take creative thinking to a new level. I would also like to thank the staff at Rockport Publishers for their continued support and cooperation.

This book is dedicated to my three daughters, Jen, Kristin, and Ashleigh, who have been blessed with their own special gifts: Jen your poetic use of language, Kristin your flair for colour and design, and Ashleigh your musical and creative abilities. I encourage you to reach for the stars and beyond, never losing sight of your deepest values.

about the author

Paula DeSimone teaches at the Museum of Fine Arts, the Fuller Museum of Art, and the DeCordova Museum of Art, all in Massachusetts. A dedicated artist as well as author, DeSimone currently heads a certificate program in Decorative Arts at the Rhode Island School of Design, C.E.

color shaper distributors

Oasis Art & Craft America
Building 2 Unit 1
Homestead Road
Belle Mead, NJ 08502, USA
Telephone: 1-908-874-3315 Fax: 1-908-874-5433

Royal Sovereign
7 St. Georges Industrial Estate
White Hart Lane
London N22 5QL, England
Telephone: 44-181-888-6888 Fax: 44-181-888-7029

OZ International
42 Chemin de la Fossette
93220 Gagny, France
Telephone: 33-1-4330-9818 Fax: 33-1-4330-9819

Daler Rowney
Wernher Von Braun Str 20
83052 Bruckmuhl, Germany
Telephone: 49-8062-70870 Fax: 49-8062-708770

Jules De Clerco
Graphic and Art Materials
Bd 6 Jacqueslaan 148
Bruxelles 1050, Belgium
Telephone: 32-2-648-2979 Fax: 32-2-640-5600

Best Art Materials AG
Postfach
Schwimmbadstrasse 45
CH-5430 Wettingen 1, Switzerland
Telephone: 41-56-430-19-19 Fax: 41-56-430-19-15

National Art Materials
43 Burgess Road
Bayswater
3153 Victoria, Australia
Telephone: 54-1-982-7847 Fax: 54-1-981-6225

Talens Japan Co. Ltd
1-6-20 Morinomiya Chuo.
Chuo-ku
Osaka, 540 Japan
Telephone: 81-6-910-8811 Fax: 91-6-910-8836

Heyco S.A.
J D Perron 4466
(1199) Buenos Aires, Argentina
Telephone: 54-1-982-7847 Fax: 54-1-981-6225

Americo De Araujo Barbosa
Rua Do Barao De S. Cosme
184-178 4000 Porto, Portugal
Telephone: 351-2519-3490 Fax: 351-2519-3493

A D I T
Via Segrino 8
20098 Sesto Ulteriano
Milan, Italy
Telephone: 39-2-982-81241 Fax: 39-2-982-81732

Talens Espana 5A
Poligono Gran Via Sur
C/Salvador Espriu 5-7
Hospitalet De Llobregat
08908 Barcelona, Spain
Telephone: 34-93-3368-750 Fax: 34-93-3368-7545

Art Media Inc.
57 Alley 30 Lane 428
Chung Chen Road
Yung Ho, Taiwan 234
Telephone: 886-2-2929-8390 Fax: 886-2-2927-8001

Hobby OG Kunst A/S
Sandakerveien 102,P.O.Box 45
Grefsen 0409 Oslo, Norway
Telephone: 47-22-7100-30 Fax: 47-22-7121-67

Paleda AB
Fabriksvagen 86
176 71 Jarfallana, Sweden
Telephone: 46-8-5835-0130 Fax: 46-8-5835-0021

Milford Britannia
Postboks 72
Vangede Bygrade 126
2820 Gentofte, Denmark
Telephone: 45-4497-1099

Argepa Limited
H. Yaghansel Sokak
Kalkavan Cem Han No2
Kat 2-3, 80320 Halicioglu
Istanbul, Turkey
Telephone: 90-212-235-9211 Fax: 90-212-256-3652

Dragon Trading Co. Ltd.
62,64 Soi Bangkwang
New Rd, Dwang Watpryakrai
Khet Bangkholaem
Bangkok 10120, Thailand
Telephone: 66-289-3545 Fax: 66-228-93500

Panno N. Color
Barabas U. 25
1107 Budapest, Hungary
Telephone: 36-1-262-9359 Fax: 36-1-260-0450

Tempera Oy
Uudenmaankatu 16-20
00120 Helsinki, Finland
Telephone: 358-9-645-916 Fax: 358-9-645-009

Ashley & Radmore (Pty) Ltd.
PO Box 57324
Springfield, 2137 South Africa
Telephone: 27-11-493-6509 Fax: 27-11-493-0445

Colart B.V.
Vlierbaan 13 2903 LR
Capelle a/d
Ljssel, Nederland
Telephone: 31-10458-0311 Fax: 31-10458-0610